THE AFFIRMATION
30 Days
POWER. HEALING. PURPOSE

Dr. Sheika Square

Priority Writing Approach
New Orleans

Copyright © 2017 Sheika Square

All rights reserved. In accordance with the U.S. Copyright Act of 1976, the scanning, uploading, and electronic sharing of any part of this book without the permission of the publisher constitutes unlawful piracy and theft of the author's intellectual property. If you would like to use material from this book (other than for review purposes), prior written permission must be obtained by contacting the publisher. Thank you for your support of the author's rights.

Priority Writing Approach
P.O. Box 872952
New Orleans, LA 70122

www.drsheikasquare.com

The publisher is not responsible for websites (or their content) that are not owned by the publisher.

Copy Editor: Lynel Johnson Washington
Cover Design: Dr. Sheika Square
Photograph: Harlan Breaux

All rights reserved.

ISBN: 0-9986290-3-0
ISBN-13: 978-0-9986290-3-2

Many people get caught in the struggle of perfection, misunderstanding that they are already lacking nothing and have already attained rightness.

Once you accept this perspective, you begin to see life differently...more completely. Dreams manifest from your wholeness and purpose radiates from every part of your being. There is only one way to walk out of pain… and that's by walking toward your purpose.

Be exquisite. Be unique. Be unapologetically you.

-Dr. Sheika Square

CONTENTS

	ACKNOWLEDGMENTS	i
1	PURPOSE	1
2	HEALING	23
3	POWER	39

ACKNOWLEDGMENTS

With love, healing, and deliverance.

THE AFFIRMATION

Dr. Sheika Square

THE AFFIRMATION
30 Days
POWER. HEALING. PURPOSE.

Dr. Sheika Square

PURPOSE.

Dr. Sheika Square

THE AFFIRMATION

I will remember my perfection and forgive all of my flaws.

Dr. Sheika Square

THE AFFIRMATION

Everyone has a purpose.

Dr. Sheika Square

I am not a mistake.

Dr. Sheika Square

I am my truth and my wisdom.

Dr. Sheika Square

I will remove fear and embrace the unknown.

Dr. Sheika Square

THE AFFIRMATION

Time does not wait for me, so I will get ahead of time.

Dr. Sheika Square

THE AFFIRMATION

I will accept the rejections and embrace the difficulties in my life.

If rejection is too difficult for you to handle, you don't understand your destiny.

Dr. Sheika Square

I will understand that my life mimics my choices.

Success has always fallen victim to those who are unwilling to give up on their dreams.

Dr. Sheika Square

THE AFFIRMATION

I will pursue more because I deserve it.

Dr. Sheika Square

THE AFFIRMATION

I am fearless.

In an effort to be great you must release all fear.

Dr. Sheika Square

HEALING.

Dr. Sheika Square

THE AFFIRMATION

I believe in myself.

Dr. Sheika Square

THE AFFIRMATION

I will distance myself from the wrong people in an attempt to make room for the right people.

Dr. Sheika Square

I am okay with being alone.

It is foolish to think that the friends you had before, will stay your friends now that you are different...better. Accepting singleness in your personal life, allows a reawakening of your own creativity.

Dr. Sheika Square

THE AFFIRMATION

I will keep my heart and hands open.

Regardless of what happened, it's impossible to experience joy, passion, or real love, while focusing on hate, un-forgiveness, and pain.

Dr. Sheika Square

THE AFFIRMATION

I am worthy of love.

In an effort to receive love, you must first be open to it.

Dr. Sheika Square

THE AFFIRMATION

I will learn to be my own best friend.

Dr. Sheika Square

THE AFFIRMATION

I am love and full of love.

Dr. Sheika Square

POWER.

Dr. Sheika Square

I will live a life that is peaceful and fulfilling.

Dr. Sheika Square

THE AFFIRMATION

This life is too short to also be impossible.

Sometimes I wonder if we are going to keep complaining about the way things are or are we going to take action. Instead of sitting on the sidelines, get out and make life happen. Be the doer in your life, the doer that gets exactly what you want.

Dr. Sheika Square

I will let my light shine.

The most important thing about being alive is that you get to be you. There is no one else alive that looks just like you! No one else has your purpose. No one else has your *swag*. No one else can do that thing that you do, the way that you do it. Whenever you're feeling a little confused about who and what you are, remember that you were put here to be just like you and it's so important to be unique.

Dr. Sheika Square

I will see myself as I am and not as others want me to be.

It is so important for you to love yourself. Self-love is the foundation of every relationship; the relationship you have with yourself, the relationship you have with your partner, the relationship you have with your family.

A feeling of self-worth is also important for self-esteem. Learn to love and accept yourself.

Dr. Sheika Square

THE AFFIRMATION

I will speak with power.

Dr. Sheika Square

I am happy where I am.

It is important to formulate happiness in your present situation...

Dr. Sheika Square

THE AFFIRMATION

I will live a life that changes me.

Live in the light and watch your life change.

Dr. Sheika Square

I will give more than I take.

Dr. Sheika Square

THE AFFIRMATION

I will choose what defines me.

Your response matters more than any obstacle, any downfall, or any troubling situation. Choose what will define you.

Dr. Sheika Square

I will stay committed to my dreams.

Stress comes in to distract you. Purpose is usually on the other side of it. Giving up is not a weakness, however, giving up on your dreams leaves you without purpose. Think about what it is you are risking if you give up. Think about what you could gain if you stick with it.

Dr. Sheika Square

I will champion my triumphs and forgive my failures.

Dr. Sheika Square

In this hopeless time I am an anomaly; for I am hopeful and hoping.

Dr. Sheika Square

THE AFFIRMATION

This is my time.

Dr. Sheika Square

The End

Dr. Sheika Square

THE AFFIRMATION

Bonus Excerpt From *21 Day Word Revolution: Stop Living the Life You Hate and Start Living the Life of Your Dreams*

Dr. Sheika Square

Text copyright ©2017 by Sheika Square

My Words Have Power
So What Power Have I Given Them?

Look around you and see your words. The phone you have, the spouse you live with, the person you date, the car you drive, the job you have, all attracted to you by you. Now ask yourself if these are the possessions/people you want or just what you thought you could have? In order to answer that fully, you must first examine the ideals and many times false beliefs given to you in your childhood. Whether it was your biological parents, step parents, adoptive parents, single parents, or family/friends that step in as parents, teachers, mentors, store clerks, or choir teachers, a series of ideals were handed down to you shaping your approach to life by shaping the thoughts that have created your words. Through these teachings or ideals, you learned a plethora of fallacies, misnomers, erroneous coping skills, and a host of patterns, that highlighted a path to your current reality. As a result, many people (like my former self) clumsily muddle through life, making one destructive statement after another; causing one wrong decision after another.

Knowing this, however, does absolutely nothing for you. Changing it does wonders. We all know that our parents did the best they could, but still neglected many intricate details about the power of words. I am sure right now, you are thinking about all the words you said to yourself just yesterday. Even if you are a "positive thinker", you may still not have the life you want because of the words that follow your thoughts. By making small adjustments to the words you say, you can both immediately and positively impact the trajectory and the circumstances surrounding your life.

Do you ever remember saying any of the following, especially when you were naïve and child-like?

"I will become a doctor."

"I will marry a basketball player."
(me…)

"I want to live with my mother for the rest of my life."

"When I'm older I'm going to do whatever I want."

> *"When I'm older, I'm going to have all the shoes I want."*

Now examine your current reality and think about how many of these things came true. I am not talking about the things you said and forgot. I am talking about words uttered with true conviction. In my youth, I used to tell everyone I would become a doctor one day. My youngest memory of discussing a career path is steeped firmly in becoming a doctor. Low and behold, I am writing this book and speaking all around the world as Dr. Sheika Square. The power of words is absolutely amazing.

We can even examine this on a simpler level. Do you ever remember saying, after putting on those new, must-have black leather, perfectly designed, half-a-paycheck pair of shoes, "I hope I don't trip in these or get them scratched up?" What happened? You not only tripped but got the biggest scuff mark right across the front. This is because your words only work with the universe (the energy around you, the energy connected to a higher source, being at its highest level) to validate you. You say *I hope I **don't** trip,* but the universe hears I hope I trip in these or get them scratched up. The universe then attracts the biggest hole in the sidewalk or crack in the stairs, while making your phone ring at the same time, to help draw in the energy you put out there. Imagine working with this energy, with the universe, to get exactly what you want and have the best life possible.

Dr. Sheika Square

21-DAY WORD REVOLUTION

ABOUT THE AUTHOR

Dr. Sheika Square is one of this generation's pioneering leaders and captivating speakers. Along with the knowledge to make solutions and complex resolutions elucidated, Dr. Sheika Square's ability to connect with her audience and move them to action is unparalleled. Her work as a financial consultant and leader in the fields of Leadership and Education adds to her ability to disseminate information that enhances the lives of others. With over 10 years of experience in Leadership and Education, many would say that Dr. Square not only empowers, but sets the standard of what it means to inspire.

NOTES

NOTES

NOTES

Made in the USA
Lexington, KY
21 March 2018